How to Position Your Retirement Nest Egg to Ensure you Don't Run Out of Money

Without knowing a thing about finances

DAN CASEY

ISBN: 978-1-4834-9030-4 (sc)
ISBN: 978-1-4834-9031-1 (hc)
ISBN: 978-1-4834-9029-8 (e)

Rev. date: 12/28/2018

To my lovely wife, Nina, and three beautiful children, Sean, Jade, and Nick who make it all worthwhile. Thank you. Without your support and patience, I would have never achieved my dream.

Contents

Social Security..5

Pensions 15

The Gap..21

Rollover Discussion 25

Long Term Care Protection..29

Strategies To Fill The Gap..41

Estate Planning 55

Medicaid planning 61

I thought it was time to write a book to address my process of putting together how I plan the best retirement plan for each prospect that comes into my office. Before I start, let me briefly take you back to my life as a 12-year-old boy growing up in the small town of Imlay City, about an hour North of Detroit, Michigan. Farming and crops were abundant, and we had two stop lights.

You can ask any of my family members how saving money while working was important to me. The idea of getting interest on my money while letting the bank 'borrow' it was just about more than I could take – I was in love and I was a saver. I bought my family our first VCR. The big decision was either Beta or VHS. I chose VHS because the video store had a wider selection of VHS and I wasn't convinced Beta was the upcoming trend. It turned out I was right. I believe the core of my decision was purely because my Dad was pushing for Beta and of course, I wanted to do the opposite.

I bought mostly all my new school clothes and I also bought my first car, however, it was actually a van. And it was clear, although I had no direct knowledge at the time, that I was attempting to see how much garbage you could fit in the back of an orange, rusty Ford Van with a Windsor 350.

The first job I remember was answering multiple phone lines for various businesses and taking messages. I was 11 years old and had no business answering phones. But who was I to turn down an opportunity to make $1.50 an hour? While sitting in the small, dingy office building I noticed the parking lot of a neighboring business was filthy. I offered to sweep it once a week for ten dollars. One day, while my friend was visiting me as I swept, the next business over noticed my fine sweeping skills and wanted their parking lot swept also. However, the job was offered to both my friend and I. Even though I wasn't very happy about sharing my earnings, I must admit, I did enjoy the company.

When I would walk home from my day of sweeping I would notice a few homes for sale and how their yards were not well kept. I remember thinking the houses might sell faster if the lawns were cut. I immediately called the Real Estate Agents to offer my lawn cutting services.

They agreed instantly and no contact between them and I ever occurred again. Checks for $10 started arriving to my house on a weekly basis for each house I was cutting – no questions asked. I believe this is when my love of recurring income began.

To this day, I still eagerly walk to the mailbox with the excitement of that 12-year-old boy somewhere in the back of my mind. I'll never forget that great feeling of being paid for a hard day's work.

After high school, I went to Oakland University in Auburn Hills, Michigan and received by undergraduate degree in Economics. Afterwards, I received a master's Degree in Finance from Walsh College in Troy, Michigan. With that love of recurring income still present, I bought my first home when I was 28 and then another by age 30 and continued to buy about a home a year. The purpose was to fix them up and rent them out. I even ventured into the Great White North and bought a home in Canada on Lake Huron.

I met my beautiful wife, Nina, a Family Practice Physician during her residency in 1999. We built our first home which is where we brought home our three children; Sean, Jade, and Nicholas. As I write this they are 14, 12, and 9 respectively. They are the loves of my life and every day they remind me of what's important. I try my best to 'say as I do' and 'do as I say' because I know that even though they don't hear everything I say, my actions and how I treat other people is just as important.

While getting my degrees, I worked for NBD, which then became First Chicago NBD, which then became Bank One. During all the mergers and acquisitions, my growth in the company wasn't happening as fast as I would have liked. So, I quit and began working at a day trading firm in West Bloomfield. Several years later, soon after March of 2000, the company wasn't doing that well. The tech bubble had burst. At some point investors all agreed, as if on one grand conference call, that the rising stock prices were based on speculation and not fundamentals. The stock market plunged, and many companies went bankrupt. Some went away never to be seen again.

I was laid off soon after and was left to determine my next step in my career. It didn't take me long to figure out that a Financial Advisor was my best move. I had already received my series 7, 63, 55 and 24 which were the necessary licenses to buy and sell stocks and mutual funds for clients, manage employees and to be a Principal of the Firm. The intense studying and difficulty of those tests stick with me to this day. I couldn't let my licenses lapse and I couldn't ignore my love of money, investing and helping individuals. So, it was an easy decision.

The beginning years were a struggle. Nina had since graduated and was working full time as a doctor. Once we started a family, the hours in the day became shorter and shorter as we did our best to divide our time between work and family. My company, whose name started out different and has since taken on many forms, is now Bridgeriver Advisors. Growth was slow in the beginning but with persistence and the belief there was no other option, I continued. My firm is now in Bloomfield Hills, Michigan where I can offer a boutique service to retirees with attorneys offering Estate Planning, Business Law, Tax Planning, and residential and commercial real estate needs.

SOCIAL SECURITY

L et's now begin to build your rock-solid retirement plan. Our first step is to calculate the guaranteed income you'll have when you do retire. The first guaranteed income we'll analyze is social security. In order to do that, you first want to determine what your full retirement age is according to the Social Security Administration. The table below shows how to figure that out. If you were born between 1943 and 1954 like most of my clients, it will be 66.

Full Retirement Ages

If you were born in:	Your full retirement age is:
1943-1954	66
1955	66 and 2 months
1956	66 and 4 months
1957	66 and 6 months
1958	66 and 8 months
1959	66 and 10 months
1960 and later	67

We'll get into why you need to know your full retirement age in just a minute. As you can see, for every subsequent year later than 1954—the year you were born—you increase it by two months. Hence in 1960 and later, it's 67.

How do you figure out how much Social Security you'll receive at your full retirement age?

There's a couple of ways you can do it. That full retirement age is when you receive your primary insurance amount (PIA), and you can get that from www.socialsecurity.gov or statements in the mail. On the www.socialsecurity.gov website, you will click the bottom left corner labeled, "my Social Security". They'll go through a verification process, when that is completed, you'll be able to determine what your PIA is or what you'll receive at your full retirement age.

During the great recession, the Administration stopped mailing statements because it was too expensive. They have recently started mailing them every five years. You should have received one recently; if not, go online and find out what your primary insurance amount (PIA) is.

As you can see, according to the chart below, we're going to assume that your full retirement age is 67. If you look at that arrow on the left-hand side, it says full retirement age or FRA. The age of 67 is your full retirement age; that's when you'll get 100% of your full retirement amount. On the left-hand column, you can see your benefit reduction or increase; if you take it earlier than 67, it reduces. At 66, it will be 93.33% of your full retirement amount, and then it decreases to 70% of your PIA if you take it as early as 62. You can't take it any earlier unless there is a disability or your widowed.

As you can see, once you exceed your full retirement age, your benefits increase by 8%; called delayed retirement credits (DRC). If you can delay taking your social security benefits past your full retirement age, 67 in this example, your benefits increase by 8% a year. I'm going to show you exactly how to calculate to see if that makes sense for you.

Your Own Benefit Reduction/Increase	Your Age
70%	62
75%	63
80%	64
86.66%	65
93.33%	66
100%	67
108%	68
116%	69
124%	70

FRA

Delayed
Retirement
Credits – 8%

Remember, if you take it as early as 62, it will be reduced forever. At that point, you'll only receive COLA raises, cost of living adjustments. If you've been receiving your benefits for less than 12 months, you can stop your social security checks and then resume it whenever you want, up to 70. If you chose to do this before your full retirement age, you'll have to pay back the benefits you've received for that period. If you decide to do this after your full retirement age, then you do not have to pay back your benefits.

If you do delay your benefits, you don't have to wait until that full year is up to get that full 8% delayed retirement credits. It will be prorated.

Strategies that remain for married and divorced couples:

As you might be aware, file and suspend, which is a strategy I would do for my clients quite a bit, is gone now. In one week's time, it was there, and then it was gone. A strategy they didn't eliminate but just phased out is called restricted application. When you normally file for social security benefits, you are filing for the highest benefit that you're deemed to receive, which is either 100% of your own benefit, 50% of your spousal benefit, or 50% of a divorced spouse's benefit (if applicable). When you're filing a restricted application, you're telling the Social Security Administration that you do not want the Administration to review all the benefits that are available to you. You want a specific benefit—meaning not your own. Instead, you are asking for your spousal benefit that you're allowed to receive. What this allows you to do is, while your own benefits will continue to increase by 8% a year with DRC's, you are getting your spousal benefit. Because it's being phased out, you need to be born before January 2, 1954, to take advantage of this and you must have reached your full retirement age. By filing a restricted application at your full retirement age, instructing the Administration that you want your spousal benefit; it will not affect your own benefit. In fact, your own benefit will continue to increase by 8% a year while you're receiving your spousal benefits. It's powerful if you can do it. Let's go over an example.

In the figure below, we have a married couple. For this example, the lower wage-earning spouse is the wife, and the higher wage earner is the husband. Let's say the lower wage-earning spouse is 62, and the higher

wage earner is 66. With this age spread, it happens to work out perfect; there are other age spreads where it can work as well, but in this example, the lower wage-earning spouse would file right away at 62. That's because the higher wage-earning spouse, because he's at his full retirement age, can file a restricted application and get the spousal benefit or half of his wife's benefits, which she's now receiving. And while he's receiving this 50% spousal benefit, his own benefits are increasing by 8% a year. It doesn't affect her benefits at all- she's getting her full benefits. It *is* reduced because she took it at 62, before her full retirement age. Let's look at that a little bit more in the Figure pictured below.

Total benefits of $4,554 a month with this strategy as opposed to $3,533 a month without. Plus the older spouse received $500 a month for four years ($24,000)

Let's say the benefits of the lower wage-earning spouse amounted to $1,333 per month at her full retirement age. And for the higher wage-earning spouse, let's say his was $2,200 per month at his age 66, his full retirement. If you go right below that, let's say she files at 62, she starts getting $1,000 a month. See how it's reduced by approximately

30%? Had she waited till 66, she would have received $1,333 as her primary insurance amount. But she's going to get $1,000 because she took it early. But now let's go over to the husband at 66; he's going to file a restricted application telling the Administration he does not want his own benefits, he wants his spousal benefit—so, 50% of her benefits. Now he's going to get $500 a month while he lets his own benefits increase by 8% a year.

She's going to continue to get that $1,000 a month from age 63 through 65, and if there are COLA or cost of living adjustments, those will be included. If you jump back over to his columns, he's going to continue to get that $500 a month until he turns age 70, and then he's going to switch to his own benefits based on his own earnings record that has now increased by 32%.

If you see his primary insurance amount at 66, he would have received $2,200 a month, but he waited, so now he's going to get $2,904 a month. That $500 a month for four years would have been missed if you didn't know about the strategy of filing a restricted application.

What she's going to do at her full retirement age is, because his benefits are so large, she's going to now switch over to her spousal benefit, which is 50% of his primary insurance amount. It's confusing because it's not exactly 50% of what he's going to get at 70 because, remember, she did take her benefits early. Any benefits going forward that she takes will be reduced by that same percentage amount that her benefits decreased because she took it early.

The total benefits of $4,554 a month is what they'll both get now that's she's 66 and he's 70. They would have only received $3,533 had they just taken them at their full retirement age. Also, the older spouse receives $500 a month for four years or about $24,000 while he was letting his benefits increase.

Using restricted application for divorced couples:

Assuming you meet the birthday requirement, and you are at your full retirement age, you may be able to get divorced spousal benefits. If you were married for at least 10 years you can file a restricted application. If you've been divorced for more than two years, then that ex-spouse doesn't even need to have filed for social security benefits for you to get your spousal benefits. You can't be remarried, and the spouse must be at least 62 years of age. It doesn't affect your ex-spouse's social security benefits. This is a separate bucket; in fact, you don't even need to contact him or her. Tax statements from previous years, when you were married, should suffice.

While you're getting your ex-spouse's social security spousal benefits, your own benefits will increase with the delayed retirement credits of 8% a year. One issue is, if you're not born before January 2, 1954, you can no longer file a restricted application—meaning you cannot get your ex-spouse's benefits while allowing your own benefits to increase. You still have access to your divorced spouses benefits but if your own benefits are higher than 50% of your divorced spouses benefits then there is no way to get your divorced spouses benefits while letting your benefits increase. A very unfortunate aspect of the law that passed. I don't think that was the intention of the law and I'm hoping it will be changed. Presidents Trump's new plan didn't address it.

Let's look at the divorced benefits in a little more detail using the graphic below.

Let's say the ex-spouse's primary insurance is $1,333 at 62. She hasn't yet filed for social security and the divorce was over two years ago.

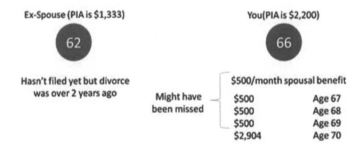

Let's say she's 66, and her primary insurance amount is $2,200. She'll file a restricted application, get $500 spousal benefit (less than 50% of his PIA) for the ex-spouse because he has not reached his full retirement age. Her own benefits will increase to $2,904 to age 70. She'll then switch to her own benefits.

You may ask yourself if there is some breakeven where waiting doesn't make sense anymore. There's a general idea here: whether you take it at 62, 66, 70, the break-even seems to be in the high 70s, low 80s, which can be seen on the graphic below. Of course, nobody knows how long we're going to live. If you have bad genes in your family and you don't think you're going to live a long life, then maybe, taking it right away makes sense. Most advisors say try to delay it, but that's not always the answer, is it? Sometimes you want to just take it now, and this breakeven chart shows why. However, look at those bar charts at the bottom; they are larger beyond that break-even of 78.

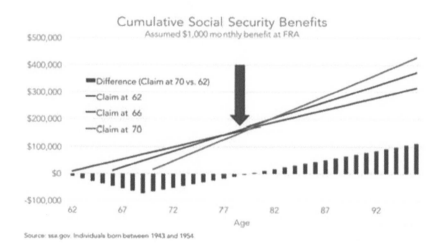

retirement age. She'll then switch to her own benefits.

That's the difference between had you taken it as early, as you could at 62, or waited till 70. You can see, if you live into your high 80s, it's a substantial amount. In your 90s, it's approximately $100,000 difference that ended up in your pocket had you lived that long.

If you don't think you're going to live past 78 then take it early. The problem with this break-even point is, it does not take into effect the restricted application strategy. This just attempts to answer the question whether to take your benefits early or wait but not had you filed the restricted application. Using the restricted application strategy can add additional benefit amounts, skewing the breakeven point.

Things to consider when taking social security

So, if you do decide to postpone receiving social security, do you have other assets to replace the income if your retired? If you have enough assets in your portfolio, you may be able to build some dividends and investments that will produce income to match what your benefits would be, so that you can let your social security grow. Sometimes that may be a good idea because social security benefits are taxed differently than ordinary income. Benefits can be either tax exempt, only 50% of your benefits are taxable or as high as 85% of your benefits are taxable, whereas money coming out of your IRAs has usually never been taxed so 100% of it will be taxable. It's not always a bad idea to take some of that money out of your IRA while you let your social security benefits increase because your social security benefits can be taxed at a much lower rate.

If you're taking benefits before your full retirement age, and you work, your benefits will be reduced. If you live long enough, they will be added back to your record, and you'll get it all back. If you're at your full retirement age, then it doesn't matter. You can work as much as you want, and your social security will not be affected. Contact the administration if you would like to work in the same year in which you reach your full retirement age because there are some calculations that will need to be done.

An important point to remember is, if you're married, the larger social security check will remain for both lives. So, delaying it might be the best. This is a big takeaway I try to get people at my seminars to understand. Try to get the higher wage earners check as high as possible by delaying it. Again, let's assume it's the husband. His social security check will not only be for him, but when he dies, it becomes the wife's social security. She'll lose her social security and start receiving his benefit amount. That higher social security amount is for both of their lives—for the rest of their lives. So, it's important to get the higher wage earners check as high as possible.

Married couples should try and use the restricted application strategy to get the higher wage earner benefits higher. Single retirees should also use a restricted application for their spousal benefit if divorced and meet the criteria. Delaying it greatly depends on other assets in your portfolio to replace the social security that is being delayed. We will discuss this in greater detail in coming chapters.

PENSIONS

To begin constructing an income plan, let's start with our fictitious retirees, Jim and Betty, ages 66 and 62 respectively. You can create this in a spreadsheet program or on paper. Suppose Jim's social security's will be $6,000 a year. He'll receive that spousal benefit while his own benefits increase. Betty's social security is $1,000 a month, so she's going to receive $12,000 a year, and then it continues each year until Jim reaches 70. He'll switch to his own benefits, now at $34,848, and then Betty's will receive her spousal benefit.

Jim's Age	Betty's Age	Jim's SS	Betty's SS				
66	62	$6,000	$12,000				
67	63	$6,000	$12,000				
68	64	$6,000	$12,000				
69	65	$6,000	$12,000				
70	66	$34,848	$19,800				

Let's next discuss pensions. We want to calculate the rollover options (if they're available) and compare them to pension payments. When you have a pension, you usually have two options. You can take it as a lump sum (which means a tax-free rollover to an IRA) or you can take it in annuity payments. Payments can be set up to get paid to you and your spouse for the rest of your lives.

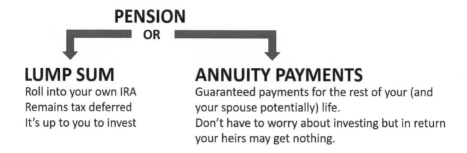

PENSION
OR

LUMP SUM
Roll into your own IRA
Remains tax deferred
It's up to you to invest

ANNUITY PAYMENTS
Guaranteed payments for the rest of your (and your spouse potentially) life.
Don't have to worry about investing but in return your heirs may get nothing.

What are the main differences?

Lump sum: Your able to roll your pension into your own IRA.

I still meet people today who are not aware that, if you're able to roll your pension out, it is a tax-free event. You roll your pension into your own IRA; there are no taxes owed. But now that it's in an IRA, if you take money out, it's going to be taxed at your own income tax level. The major benefit is, when you roll it into your own IRA, it remains tax-deferred. Just like it was while you were working. But the difficult part, maybe for some, is that it's up to you to invest it.

Annuity payments: The pros are guaranteed payments for the rest of your life and the life of your spouse depending on which option you pick. This option is guaranteed and takes away any worries you may have when it comes to investing the money on your own. A con to the annuity payment route means your heirs may get nothing in return. You may pick payments guaranteed for your life and your spouse's, but if you both die a month later, no one's getting that money anymore unless you chose something that's called 'term certain' with your pension company. But, in doing so, your pension payments will be reduced. So the tradeoff for receiving guaranteed payments for the rest of your life are the benefits may be gone when you and your spouse die. What's important to know is every option that's better for you reduces your annuity payments. So, you don't have to worry about investing, but in turn, the heirs may get nothing.

If you take the annuity payment option, determine which spousal option works best and know what the time certain option equates to. For example, in the figure on the next page, you may have three decisions. The first one is, you can receive $1,000 a month right now and it will continue for spouse A, and then you can see, at the end of that blue line; spouse A dies, and then spouse B will continue to get that $1,000 a month, and then spouse B dies, the payment ends.

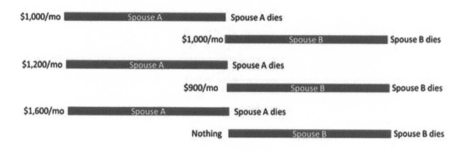

The next option is, the pension company will give you a higher monthly benefit. Your pension payments will be $1,200 a month. Spouse A will get that amount until spouse A dies, but because you receive more upfront, spouse B only receives $900 a month for the rest of their life until they die. The third option might be $1,600 a month for spouse A, but when spouse A dies, spouse B gets nothing. Why would you do that? What if you take the first option, $1,000 a month for five years and spouse B predeceases you? You took that lower amount for a reason that doesn't make sense anymore. Your spouse won't be receiving anything and that lower amount will remain for the rest of your life. They predeceased you, so when you die, that money is gone.

Sometimes, what I'll advise my clients to do is take the $1,600 a month, which means spouse B gets nothing when you die, but we will use the difference to cover the spouse. One option is to take the $600 a month difference and invest it in life insurance. So when spouse A dies, spouse B will get a lump sum of tax free money. Spouse A is no worse off if spouse B predeceases them. But if spouse B doesn't predecease then she has a death benefit to help with the lost income.

Time certain option—If you receive the $1,000 a month for spouse A and spouse B, and you both die soon after – all payments stop. The option of 'time certain' implies you'll receive payments for some specific time frame. That means that $1,000 a month will be paid out for a specific time period even if you both die within six months; it's going to be paid out to the beneficiaries. That'll affect the amount too. If time certain is picked, you may only get $900 a month, for example.

If you selected pension payout and not the lump sum, enter that amount on a spreadsheet or sheet of paper. On our spreadsheet, let's add in Jim's pension and when that's going to begin. Also, add in a column to address your required minimum distributions.

Jim's Age	Betty's Age	Jim's SS	Betty's SS	Jim's Pension	Jim's RMDs	Total Income
66	62	$6,000	$12,000			$18,000
67	63	$6,000	$12,000	$14,000		$32,000
68	64	$6,000	$12,000	$14,000		$32,000
69	65	$6,000	$12,000	$14,000		$32,000
70	66	$34,848	$19,800	$14,000	$30,000	$98,648

What are required minimum distributions (RMD)? The IRS says you cannot leave money lingering in tax-deferred accounts. They want their tax money. Due to IRS regulations, you cannot leave money in a tax-deferred account (Roth IRAs are an exception). At age 70 ½ you are required to withdraw a percentage of the money and pay the necessary taxes owed on all withdrawals. When the owner passes, and it goes to the spouse or other beneficiaries, each beneficiary will have rules. Beneficiaries may have to continue RMD's, begin taking RMDs, or neither if you are the spouse. Call me or consult a qualified advisor on this important aspect of IRA inheritance.

The idea is that the IRS wants these tax-deferred accounts depleted by your 'actuarial death'. Meaning if, actuarially, you should live to 91 then you must slowly take out withdrawals every year in order for your IRA to be depleted by that age. You can roughly estimate that to be about 4% of whatever the balance is of all those deferred accounts you own. If you still have a 401K or 403B at your old employer, that will get added in as well. There are some exceptions when you don't have to take out money from a company plan so contact me or a qualified advisor.

Jim's Age	Betty's Age	Jim's SS	Betty's SS	Jim's Pension	Jim's RMDs	Total Income
66	62	$6,000	$12,000			$18,000
67	63	$6,000	$12,000	$14,000		$32,000
68	64	$6,000	$12,000	$14,000		$32,000
69	65	$6,000	$12,000	$14,000		$32,000
70	66	$34,848	$19,800	$14,000	$30,000	$98,648

Approximately 4% of the addition of all your IRAs & company plans.

Many of my clients don't even want the required distribution. Their social security, pensions and/or dividend income is enough. But this income must be paid and sometimes places them into higher tax brackets. Using the spreadsheet example from before, enter the RMD of $30,000 on the spreadsheet. Again, it's approximately 4%. I added in $30,000 as an example.

THE GAP

et's next calculate what the ideal income in retirement is for most retirees. What I've found is, most retirees want to replace 100% of their preretirement income. Aspects that you want to consider: Will your mortgage be paid off? Will you purchase a second home? Do you want to travel? Whatever it is, what income do you think you need or would like in retirement? There's a rule of thumb that says your retirement income should be 70-80% of whatever your working income is in retirement. I have found retirees usually want 100% of whatever their income was during their working years.

Now we need to calculate the gap. Take your desired retirement income; subtract your social security and your pensions, and that's the income gap to be filled by your investments.

Desired Retirement Income
subtract
Social Security
subtract
Pensions
Income Gap to be filled by investments

If you've selected the pension payout, not the lump sum, enter that amount on the spreadsheet or sheet of paper because we're only discussing income at this time. If you roll out a $300,000 401K into an IRA, that's not represented on this sheet because we are currently focusing on income – not assets. In figure X we now have Jim's RMD or required minimum distribution beginning. I also added a total income column. Our updated spreadsheet is reflected on the following page. If you go down $98,648, that's the addition of all the columns before. The social security plus the pension plus the RMD. The next column is the income requirement, that is the income you would like to receive in retirement. The last column is the income gap. That's the difference between income requirement and total income receiving. If there's a gap there, we need to figure out how we're going to fill that with your investments.

Jim's Age	Betty's Age	Jim's SS	Betty's SS	Jim's Pension	Jim's RMDs	Total Income	Income Requirement	Income Gap
66	62	$6,000	$12,000			$18,000	$90,000	$72,000
67	63	$6,000	$12,000	$14,000		$32,000	$90,000	$58,000
68	64	$6,000	$12,000	$14,000		$32,000	$90,000	$58,000
69	65	$6,000	$12,000	$14,000		$32,000	$90,000	$58,000
70	66	$34,848	$19,800	$14,000	$30,000	$98,648	$90,000	($8,648)

This column is the total of the previous columns

This column subtracts 'Income Requirement' from 'Total Guaranteed Income'

ROLLOVER DISCUSSION

A rollover is when you have a company plan, like a 401K, 403B, 457, etc., and you'll usually want to roll that out into your own IRA. But let's look at the other options. As discussed, the first one is rolling your company plan into your own IRA; that will provide more control and more access, allowing you to invest in most investments. Inside a 401K, you might be limited to what you can invest in. There are creditor issues in some states, meaning creditors may be able to have access to your retirement plans. In the state where my practice is, Michigan, there are no creditor issues if it's rolled into an IRA. But there are slightly different creditor laws with money in an IRA as opposed to a 401K. 401Ks are covered under the ERISA statute. ERISA is an acronym for Employee Retirement Income Security Act (1974). Whereas IRAs are under the creditor statutes of each state, you will want to check with your state. Most are protected from creditors.

The second option is leaving it with your company. You can even roll it into your new company's plan if you didn't retire and your new employer allows it. If you ever want to take a loan from the savings then you'll want to keep it in a 401k. You cannot take a loan from an IRA. Most advisors won't show that to you because they want those assets under their control. You can also perform in-plan Roth conversions in some 401Ks so contact your plan administrator if this interests you. It would involve conversion taxes (the taxes due on the taxable rollover amount), but maybe that's something that you want to do instead of rolling into an IRA first and then into a Roth.

And then there are aspects that a lump sum distribution might allow you do that you wouldn't be able to do if rolled into an IRA. If you have highly appreciated company stock in your plan, you might want to consider a strategy called net unrealized appreciation or NUA. If you have company stock—meaning your employers stock owned inside your 401K or company plan—you can withdraw it and pay tax on the purchase price – not the current value. Had you rolled this amount into your IRA, when you retire and then withdraw this money, you'll be taxed at your regular income tax rate like all IRA distributions. There is a NUA statute in tax law that states you can roll out just the company plan stock into a brokerage account, or a non-IRA account, and then the rest of the money into an IRA. What that means is, at that time you roll out your company stock, you'll pay taxes on what you purchased it at - not the current value.

This works great, for instance, if you purchased company stock 20 years ago, and you've slowly been purchasing it over the years, you will only pay taxes on the original purchase price. For example, if you have some stock that you purchased at $5 a share, and the current value is now worth $30 a share you'll only pay taxes on the $5 per share of that stock. You'll never pay taxes again until you sell it, and then it will be at capital gains rates, not regular income rates which can, potentially be much lower. If you take advantage of this tax break, you can potentially save thousands of dollars if someone owns their own company stock and it's highly appreciated.

LONG TERM CARE PROTECTION

L ong-term Medical Protection: You could have a great plan; you rolled over your pension; you've calculated the best plan for your social security; you've made smart decisions. Then you have a major medical issue, like a stroke. You could leave the spouse at home in a dire situation if you need to go into the hospital or nursing home for an extended stay and the cost is being paid from your assets. Long-term medical protection is for medical care that's needed for an extended period. Most people aren't aware that Medicare will only pay for 100 days. So, if you're in a nursing home or some sort of facility for longer than that, you will be paying out of your retirement nest egg.

How much does it cost? If you look at the last column, nursing care, the average cost in 2016 in the United States is about $6,844. Or in a private room, $7,698 a month.

Monthly Costs: National Median (2016)

Home Health Care	Adult Day Health Center	Assisted Living Facility	Nursing Home Care
Homemaker Services	**Adult Day Health Care**	**Assisted Living Facility**	**Semi-Private Room**
2016 Cost$3,466	2016 Cost$2,068	2016 Cost$3,628	2016 Cost$6,844
Home Health Aide			**Private Room**
2016 Cost$3,553			2016 Cost$7,698

You can see how easy it would be to go through your investments quickly if you had to pay for that yourself.

What are the odds that you'll even need it?

The first column shows the odds of having a fire in your house. It's about 25%—but I guarantee you have homeowners insurance. How about the odds of getting into a car accident?

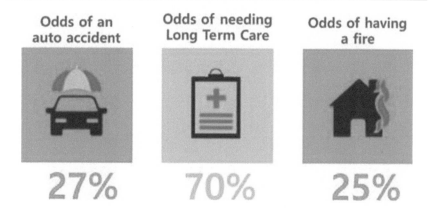

That's about 27%, but I'm sure you have auto insurance. How about the odds of needing some sort of long-term care? It's 70% and most people haven't looked into getting some sort of long term care protection.

If you do need long term care, what is the average stay?

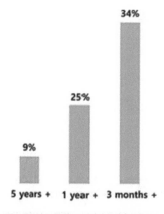

Probability of Nursing Home Use for People Turning 65 in 2020

Referring to the chart, people turning 65 in 2020 have roughly a 34% chance of staying in a nursing home facility for at least 3 months, 25% chance of staying at least 1 year and 9% chance of staying 5 years or more in a nursing home facility.

Generally, the odds are in your favor that you're not going to be in a facility for very long, but the question is, do you want to take the chance? You've worked hard your whole life to create a nest egg and a plan. Is now the time to risk a long term medical stay depleting your retirement assets? If you do have a spouse at home, they could be left with little to no assets if they are needed for your care.

What's Long-Term Care Insurance?

It's insurance that you purchase to handle these long-term care costs. The insurance usually begins paying when you cannot do two, sometimes three, activities of daily living or ADL's. This could be for care in your home or a nursing home stay.

Activities of Daily Living

1. Eating
2. Bathing
3. Dressing
4. Toileting
5. Transferring (and walking)
6. Continence

If you can't do two out of these six Activities of Daily Living, and if you have long-term care insurance, they'll start paying according to the contract.

Long-Term Care Medical Protection. What different ways can I get long-term care insurance?

The standard policy has a yearly premium. If you pay, you're covered. If you stop paying, the coverage stops. A married couple in their 60s can usually get coverage for around $3,500 a year. That'll usually pay for $100 a day, which should cover the majority but not all your expenses. You usually must wait about 90 days before the policy will begin paying. Sometimes it has inflation protection, meaning the benefits paid will rise with inflation. You can see how $100 a day might be sufficient now, but in 20 years, when you're 80 and you need it, it could potentially be worth much less with inflation. Depending on your age, you should consider this protection.

Sometimes you can pay more to have pooled benefits with your spouse. This means you can access your spouses benefits if you've exhausted yours.

Stand-alone policy: As you can see on that chart from 1990, policies were about $1,000 a year, and in 2015, the cost jumped to $2,700. Which is a substantial growth in that period.

Policy Characteristics	1990	1995	2000	2005	2010	2015
Policy type						
Nursing home only	63%	33%	14%	3%	1%	1%
Nursing home and home care	37%	61%	77%	90%	95%	96%
Home care only	—	6%	9%	7%	4%	3%
Daily benefit amount for NH care	$72	$85	$109	$142	$153	$161
Daily benefit amount for home care	$36	$78	$106	$135	$152	$155
Nursing home only elimination period	20 days	59 days	65 days	80 days	85 days	49 days
Integrated policy elimination period	——	46 days	47 days	81 days	90 days	91 days
Nursing home benefit duration	5.6 years	5.1 years	5.5 years	5.4 years	4.8 years	4.0 years
Inflation protection	40%	33%	41%	76%	74%	66%
Annual premium	$1,071	$1,505	$1,677	$1,918	$2,283	$2,727

Originally, a stand-alone policy was split between nursing home or home care. Today, it covers pretty much 100% of whatever kind of care you need. You can use it for in-home care, a nursing home facility, or anything in between. Stand-alone policies are not my favorite option due to the inevitable increasing premiums. They can become too expensive to maintain just when you need them the most.

Due to the higher premiums, I'll look at alternatives for my clients. Here's one example where it's added on as a benefit to an annuity. First, what is an annuity? Let's refer to the next picture. On the left-hand side of the picture, you can see life insurance.

Life Insurance Company Sells Both

In general terms, life insurance works where you pay small premiums every month and the life insurance will pay out a relatively huge amount at the time of your death. An annuity is essentially the other way around. You put a large amount into an annuity, and in return, you can receive smaller equal payouts for the rest of your life and the rest of your spouse's life, if chosen. Or maybe just for a certain period. Life insurance companies sell both options, and they can offer amazing benefits on both products because they're on both sides of the equation.

If they sell an annuity, the insurance company wins if you die sooner than expected. You just gave them a large premium and they don't have to pay out for a time period they expected. For life insurance, they win if you live longer because you're paying premiums for your whole life, that and they don't have to pay out a large death benefit. So insurance companies can hedge their bets by being on both sides of the equation and in doing so can offer benefits no other product can.

Types of annuities

Here are the types of annuities: (these descriptions are general and just meant to give you an idea of the various types of annuities.)

An immediate annuity: this type is similar to a pension. You deposit a lump sum of money and the annuity company will in turn pay you equal payments for the rest of your life. Instead of you having to select investments, the annuity company will guarantee payments for the rest of your life, regardless of how long you live.

A fixed annuity: A fixed annuity is similar to a certificate of deposit

(CD). You deposit a specific amount of money and the insurance company will pay, a specific flat rate. And they'll pay this for a set term, say 5 years. However, CDs are FDIC insured with the bank; annuities are not. Annuities are only guaranteed if the company is solvent and in business.

Variable annuity: That's where you place your money into an annuity, and in turn that money is invested into mutual funds. I do not like variable annuities because they're very expensive, and people don't realize just how expensive they are. And bad advisors sell bad variable annuities. People think they're getting a certain benefit, and they're not.

Index annuities: Index annuities tend to be my favorite because your money is not invested in the market. You don't have to pay mutual fund fees. The way index annuities work is that the gains are credited based on certain market indices like the S&P 500 and your principal is guaranteed. If you follow Suze Orman, in her book The Road to Wealth she states, ""**How do I know if an index annuity is right for me? If you don't want to take risk but still want to play the stock market, a good index annuity might be right for you.**"

Qualities of Annuities

Tax Deferred: Like an IRA, annuities are tax deferred meaning any profits credited to your account aren't taxed until you withdraw the money.

Guarantees: Annuities have guarantees that only insurance companies can provide. In return for certain guarantees, you have limited access to your money for a certain period. An example is, after you put your money in an annuity, you can take out 10% a year without paying any penalty. After, say 10 years, you can get all your money back, per the contract, without penalties. Every contract is different so read the fine print.

Let's look at an indexed annuity, for example. In chart on the next page, we deposited $100,000 into an indexed annuity. The figures used are hypothetical but are based on actual indexed annuities and how they are structured today.

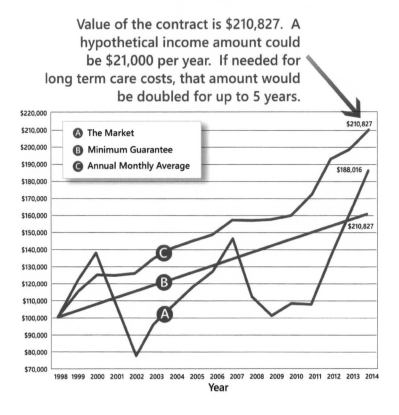

Value of the contract is $210,827. A hypothetical income amount could be $21,000 per year. If needed for long term care costs, that amount would be doubled for up to 5 years.

The A line is the stock market. The C line is how an indexed annuity can work. The B line is what the annuity would have performed had the market gone down the entire time. Or in other words, the minimum guarantee. You can see the indexed annuity value only goes up or sideways because it's participating in what the market does but your money's not actually in the market. If the market goes up, like line A does, you get a certain percentage of that, which is why the C line doesn't go up as high. Whatever gains you received, those are added to your balance and locked in. That is your new balance and it will never go lower than that. If the stock market goes up again; you get some of those returns as well. But then the market crashes are when these products shine. The locked in balance just stays the same, it won't go lower if it's locked in, which is typically either every one, two or three years. But if the market comes back, you get to participate again.

Again, referring to the chart, in the year 2002 after the market correction in 2000, the market starts to come up again and you get to participate in that. In these products, you *can* outperform the market. I would never advise someone that's what these products are designed for, but it is possible. In this example, if we put in $100,000 in this product from 1998 all the way to 2014, the value of the contract grew to $210,827. I would never put any client's money into a product that was this long but let's use this time frame as an example. The average product length is about 10 years. But in this example, let's say you put in $100,000, and at the end of the term, it was $210,000. You have the option in some of these products to then turn your balance into a pension where payments will be paid to you, and your spouse if chosen, for the rest of your life. And some of these products have no fees at all.

Let's say, in this hypothetical situation, that you wanted to turn your balance into a pension at the end of this contract and it turned out to be $21,000 a year guaranteed for the rest of your life. If you are unable to meet two of the six activities of daily living, then that income will double to $42,000 a year for five years (each contract is different). And there's no cost to that. There's no underwriting. There are no exams. That's just an added benefit that annuity companies have started to add on to sweeten the pot.

Let's review another way to get long term care insurance. Let me first illustrate how this product works in general terms. On the graph on the next page, note the 'first deposit'. In this product, you put this first deposit into a 'piggy bank' which acts almost identical to a Roth.

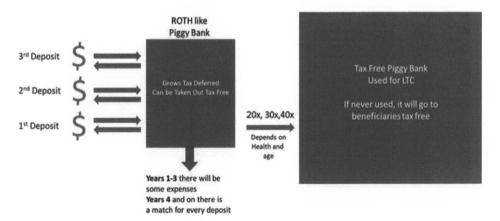

ROTH like
Piggy Bank

3rd Deposit $

2nd Deposit $

1st Deposit $

Grows Tax Deferred
Can be Taken Out Tax Free

20x, 30x, 40x
Depends on
Health and
age

Years 1-3 there will be
some expenses
Years 4 and on there is
a match for every deposit

Tax Free Piggy Bank
Used for LTC

If never used, it will go to
beneficiaries tax free

As soon as you put money in, 10 days later, you can take the balance right back out again if you want. It grows tax-deferred and it can come out tax-free. Once you put that first deposit in, the insurance company, depending on your health, will multiply that by 20, 30, or even 40 times that amount into this huge tax-free bucket noted by the bigger box on the right. That big tax-free bucket can be used for long-term care. If it's never used, it'll go to your spouse or beneficiaries completely tax-free.

If you want to continue, the second deposit will go into the Roth like piggy bank causing it to increase. The big box that's used for long-term care will also grow and it will continue to grow with each deposit. The fees are taken out in years one through three. Again, every deposit you put in grows that tax-free piggy bank on the right that can be used for long-term care and if you never need it, it can go to your spouse or beneficiaries completely tax-free. This is called a life insurance retirement plan, or LIRP, and I find you can get a lot of "bang for your buck" in these types of investments. Each dollar increases your Roth-like piggy bank and your long-term care amount which, if never used, is a death benefit.

These can be powerful products, and I suggest you either talk to me or call your financial advisor. These are whole life insurance policies that are tweaked to perform like described here.

Let's recap. We have Jim and Betty's ages, 66, 62; we have some income detailed, the income requirement and the income gap. And now we have it all protected by either using some of Jim and Betty's annual income to pay for a long-term care policy or we use some of their assets to purchase an indexed annuity with a long-term care option.

Jim's Age	Betty's Age	Jim's SS	Betty's SS	Jim's Pension	Jim's RMDs	Total Income	Income Requirement	Income Gap
66	62	$6,000	$12,000			$18,000	$90,000	$72,000
67	63	$6,000	$12,000	$14,000		$32,000	$90,000	$58,000
68	64	$6,000	$12,000	$14,000		$32,000	$90,000	$58,000
69	65	$6,000	$12,000	$14,000		$32,000	$90,000	$58,000
70	66	$34,848	$19,800	$14,000	$30,000	$98,648	$90,000	($8,648)

Or maybe we begin transferring money to a LIRP to make sure they're covered. Depending on what their asset mix is, we may want to do one or all the above. As you can see there are a number of different options and variables that can work together to customize a retirement package for you. We will get into that in more detail as we continue, but I highly recommend contacting me or seeing a financial advisor to create a package unique to your needs.

STRATEGIES TO
FILL THE GAP

W e now need to fill the gap. This is the difference between the income you want in retirement and the guaranteed income you are receiving. That gap may be filled by withdrawing from a portfolio that is invested in the stock market, annuity or dividend stocks. Dividend stocks are the classic Warren Buffett style where you're purchasing stocks that pay dividends and those dividends are what fills that gap. Your principal remains untouched. Let's examine each of these strategies.

Pros and cons of stock market

Stock market: The 'pro' for investing in the stock market is you can have massive growth. Of course, you can have massive losses as well, but the stock market is the best place if you want growth. Another 'pro' to investing in the stock market is that your portfolio is liquid. You can sell stocks at any time and use the money. However, your risk could be that the market is crashing and maybe you don't want to sell stocks at that point. If you don't know what you're doing, you run the risk of losing a lot of money. If you do hire a professional, there could be fees for their advice and for handling your stock investments, but it could be better than trying it yourself. The 'con' is sequence of returns. That is the stock broker's dirty little secret; they never want to tell people how one down market can decimate your portfolio.

Let's examine sequence of returns by looking at the following table, start at column A.

		COLUMN A			COLUMN B		
Year	Age	Beginning Amount	Yearly Return	End of Year Value	Beginning Amount	Yearly Return	End of Year Value
1	65	$500,000	18%	$590,000	$500,000	8%	$540,000
2	66	$590,000	6%	$625,400	$540,000	-16%	$453,600
3	67	$625,000	11%	$694,194	$453,600	-12%	$399,168
4	68	$694,194	5%	$728,904	$399,168	27%	$506,943
5	69	$728,904	19%	$867,395	$506,943	23%	$623,540
6	70	$867,395	-5%	$824,026	$623,540	-15%	$530,009
7	71	$824,026	18%	$972,350	$530,009	22%	$646,611
8	72	$972,350	-6%	$914,009	$646,611	18%	$763,001
9	73	$914,009	18%	$1,078,531	$763,001	-12%	$671,441
10	74	$1,078,531	23%	$1,326,593	$671,441	20%	$805,729
11	75	$1,326,593	3%	$1,366,391	$805,729	14%	$918,532
12	76	$1,366,391	11%	$1,516,694	$918,532	-6%	$863,420
13	77	$1,516,694	-5%	$1,440,859	$863,420	18%	$1,018,835
14	78	$1,440,859	31%	$1,887,525	$1,018,835	12%	$1,141,095
15	79	$1,887,525	23%	$2,321,656	$1,141,095	-6%	$1,072,630
16	80	$2,321,656	-6%	$2,182,357	$1,072,630	23%	$1,319,335
17	81	$2,182,357	12%	$2,444,240	$1,319,335	31%	$1,728,328
18	82	$2,444,240	18%	$2,884,203	$1,728,328	-5%	$1,641,912
19	83	$2,884,203	-6%	$2,711,151	$1,641,912	11%	$1,822,522
20	84	$2,711,151	14%	$3,090,712	$1,822,522	3%	$1,877,198
21	85	$3,090,712	20%	$3,708,854	$1,877,198	23%	$2,308,953
22	86	$3,708,854	-12%	$3,263,792	$2,308,953	18%	$2,724,565
23	87	$3,263,792	18%	$3,851,274	$2,724,565	-6%	$2,561,091
24	88	$3,851,274	22%	$4,698,554	$2,561,091	18%	$3,022,087
25	89	$4,698,554	-15%	$3,993,771	$3,022,087	-5%	$2,870,983
26	90	$3,993,771	23%	$4,912,339	$2,870,983	19%	$3,416,470
27	91	$4,912,339	27%	$6,238,670	$3,416,470	5%	$3,587,293
28	92	$6,238,670	-12%	$5,490,030	$3,587,293	11%	$3,981,896
29	93	$5,490,030	-16%	$4,611,625	$3,981,896	6%	$4,220,609
30	94	$4,611,625	8%	$4,980,555	$4,220,809	18%	$4,980,555

In this example, we are starting with a 65 year old investor with a portfolio of $500,000 and various yearly returns. Although this is just a hypothetical situation, the table shows roughly an 8% average return. The first 5 rows represent the market starting with some good years. Note the beginning years of returns are; 18%, 6%, 11%, 5%, and then we end with some bad or negative returns at the bottom of column A.

Let's see what happens when we have this particular sequence of returns. We start with $500,000, have some great years, now go all the way down to the bottom of the yearly return in Column A. That $500,000 grew to 4.9 million. Now go to Column B "Yearly Returns". We're going to flip every return. See how the returns at the top of Column B are now at the bottom. And note, the bottom of the Column A "Yearly Returns" is now at the top in Column B. And every return in between has been reversed. Now we start out again with some bad years in the beginning and those same awesome years at the end. We invest $500,000 and if you note at the bottom of Column B, we again have 4.9 million—makes absolutely no difference. The point being if you're not taking out income and just letting your portfolio grow, it makes no difference in the order of returns.

Here is where it gets interesting. The next table below is the same exact chart, but we're going to withdrawal $35,000 a year.

		COLUMN A			COLUMN B			
Year	Age	Beginning Amount	Yearly Return	Annual Withdrawal	End of Year Value	Beginning Amount	Yearly Return	Annual Withdrawal	End of Year Value
1	65	$500,000	18%	$35,000	$555,000	$500,000	8%	$35,000	$505,000
2	66	$555,000	6%	$36,050	$552,250	$505,000	-16%	$36,050	$388,150
3	67	$552,250	11%	$37,132	$575,866	$388,150	-12%	$37,132	$304,441
4	68	$575,866	5%	$38,245	$566,414	$304,441	27%	$38,245	$348,394
5	69	$566,414	19%	$39,393	$634,640	$348,394	23%	$39,393	$389,132
6	70	$634,640	-5%	$40,575	$562,333	$389,132	-15%	$40,575	$290,187
7	71	$562,333	18%	$41,792	$621,761	$290,187	22%	$41,792	$312,237
8	72	$621,761	-6%	$43,046	$541,410	$312,237	18%	$43,046	$325,394
9	73	$541,410	18%	$44,337	$594,527	$325,394	-12%	$44,337	$242,010
10	74	$594,527	23%	$45,667	$685,601	$242,010	20%	$45,667	$244,745
11	75	$685,601	3%	$47,037	$659,132	$244,745	14%	$47,037	$231,972
12	76	$659,132	11%	$48,448	$683,188	$231,972	-6%	$48,448	$169,605
13	77	$683,188	-5%	$49,902	$599,127	$169,605	18%	$49,902	$150,223
14	78	$599,127	31%	$51,399	$733,458	$150,233	12%	$51,399	$116,862
15	79	$733,458	23%	$52,941	$849,213	$116,862	-6%	$52,941	$56,909
16	80	$849,213	-6%	$54,529	$743,731	$56,909	23%	$54,529	$15,470
17	81	$743,731	12%	$56,165	$776,814	$15,470	31%	$56,165	($35,899)
18	82	$776,814	18%	$57,850	$858,791	($35,899)	-5%	$57,850	($91,954)
19	83	$858,791	-6%	$59,585	$747,678	($91,954)	11%	$59,585	($161,654)
20	84	$747,678	14%	$61,373	$790,980	($161,654)	3%	$61,373	($227,877)
21	85	$790,980	20%	$63,214	$885,963	($227,887)	23%	$63,214	($343,502)
22	86	$885,963	-12%	$65,110	$714,537	($343,502)	18%	$65,110	($470,443)
23	87	$714,537	18%	$67,064	$776,090	($470,443)	-6%	$67,064	($509,280)
24	88	$776,090	22%	$69,076	$877,754	($509,280)	18%	$69,076	($670,026)
25	89	$877,754	-15%	$71,148	$674,943	($670,026)	-5%	$71,148	($707,672)
26	90	$674,943	23%	$73,282	$756,898	($707,672)	19%	$73,282	($915,412)
27	91	$756,898	27%	$75,481	$885,780	($915,412)	5%	$75,481	($1,036,663)
28	92	$885,780	-12%	$77,745	$701,741	($1,036,663)	11%	$77,745	($1,228,442)
29	93	$701,741	-16%	$80,077	$509,385	($1,228,442)	6%	$80,077	($1,382,225)
30	94	$509,385	8%	$82,480	$467,656	($1,382,225)	18%	$82,480	($1,713,506)

We're even going to give ourselves a little bit of a raise and take out a little bit more the following year to keep up with inflation. So, we begin with a $500,000 portfolio and have those same great returns in the beginning. Note the bottom of the table labeled Column A, we are left with $467,000. Most investors would be ecstatic with this performance. We started with $500,000, we took out all those withdrawals every year, and we still have almost $500,000.

Here's the problem. Let's go to Column B. Same thing. Start out with $500,000; reverse all the returns. What happens at age 81? You run out of money – bankrupt! When you're not withdrawing money, it doesn't matter when the returns happen. But when you start withdrawing money, the order of returns matters a lot and it can decimate your portfolio if you have bad returns in the beginning while you're also withdrawing money. As I write this we are experiencing an incredible bull market. We could get a correction at any time. So if you are retiring now and your plan is to withdraw money from your portfolio and we do have a correction, you could run out of money much earlier than planned like the example I just illustrated.

What are some strategies to avoid this? Say your gap is $35,000 a year and your portfolio size totals $500,000. If you divide $500,000 by your $35,000 gap, you get 7%. The 7% represents the amount you could withdrawal from your accounts to get that $35,000 gap filled from a portfolio worth $500,000.

The rule of thumb is a stock market portfolio has a potential of working if the gap percentage is roughly 3%. As the percentage increases, the chances that you could deplete your portfolio does as well. There's a sequence of returns calculator that you can visit to go through your figures. You can click reset, and it completely randomizes the figures of the stock market to find out if you could possibly run out of money. Google 'sequence of returns calculator' or visit http://www.cornerstonefa.com/sequence-of-returns-calculator.8.htm.

If you don't want to touch your principal at all and only fill that gap with dividends, then the gap percentage can be roughly around 6% because that is roughly the average that dividends pay. Just remember, dividend portfolios are made up of companies that are paying you in the form of dividends, they are not using it to invest back in their companies. So growth of a dividend portfolio will not grow as fast as a pure growth portfolio made up of companies that are using excess profits and putting it back in the company in an effort to fuel growth and not paying it out in dividends.

Note my previous sequence of returns example, I used 7% as the withdraw rate. If you're taking 7% out, there's a high chance that it could decimate your portfolio if you're taking it out when the market's going down.

What if, while the years the stock market were going down, you just took money out of that tax-free Roth like piggy bank that we discussed in an earlier chapter. Remember, you can withdrawal that money tax free and as long as you leave at least $10, your tax-free bucket of long term care money stays intact.

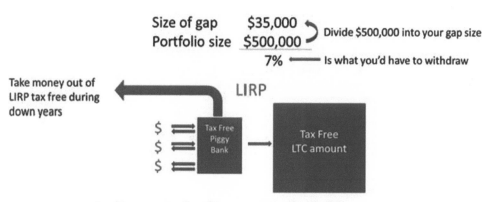

http://www.cornerstonefa.com/Sequence-of-Returns-Calculator.8.htm

Let's look at how that would work. In the following table, note all the negative years under Column B "Yearly Returns". What if we had money in the market in any of those down years and we just took our withdrawals out of the LIRP instead? You'll have to do some number crunching to see if this works.

		COLUMN A				COLUMN B		
Year	Age	Beginning Amount	Yearly Return	Annual Withdrawal	End of Year Value	Beginning Amount	Yearly Return	Annual Withdrawal	End of Year Value
1	65	$500,000	18%	$35,000	$555,000	$500,000	8%	$35,000	$505,000
2	66	$555,000	6%	$36,050	$552,250	$505,000	-16%	$36,050	$388,150
3	67	$552,250	11%	$37,132	$575,866	$388,150	-12%	$37,132	$304,441
4	68	$575,866	5%	$38,245	$566,414	$304,441	27%	$38,245	$348,394
5	69	$566,414	19%	$39,393	$634,640	$348,394	23%	$39,393	$389,132
6	70	$634,640	-5%	$40,575	$562,333	$389,132	-15%	$40,575	$290,187
7	71	$562,333	18%	$41,792	$621,761	$290,187	22%	$41,792	$312,237
8	72	$621,761	-6%	$43,046	$541,410	$312,237	18%	$43,046	$325,394
9	73	$541,410	18%	$44,337	$594,527	$325,394	-12%	$44,337	$242,010
10	74	$594,527	23%	$45,667	$685,601	$242,010	20%	$45,667	$244,745
11	75	$685,601	3%	$47,037	$659,132	$244,745	14%	$47,037	$231,972
12	76	$659,132	11%	$48,448	$683,188	$231,972	-6%	$48,448	$169,605
13	77	$683,188	-5%	$49,902	$599,127	$169,605	18%	$49,902	$150,223
14	78	$599,127	31%	$51,399	$733,458	$150,233	12%	$51,399	$116,862
15	79	$733,458	23%	$52,941	$849,213	$116,862	-6%	$52,941	$56,909
16	80	$849,213	-6%	$54,529	$743,731	$56,909	23%	$54,529	$15,470
17	81	$743,731	12%	$56,165	$776,814	$15,470	31%	$56,165	($35,899)
18	82	$776,814	18%	$57,850	$858,791	($35,899)	-5%	$57,850	($91,954)
19	83	$858,791	-6%	$59,585	$747,678	($91,954)	11%	$59,585	($161,654)
20	84	$747,678	14%	$61,373	$790,980	($161,654)	3%	$61,373	($227,877)
21	85	$790,980	20%	$63,214	$885,963	($227,887)	23%	$63,214	($343,502)
22	86	$885,963	-12%	$65,110	$714,537	($343,502)	18%	$65,110	($470,443)
23	87	$714,537	18%	$67,064	$776,090	($470,443)	-6%	$67,064	($509,280)
24	88	$776,090	22%	$69,076	$877,754	($509,280)	18%	$69,076	($670,026)
25	89	$877,754	-15%	$71,148	$674,943	($670,026)	-5%	$71,148	($707,672)
26	90	$674,943	23%	$73,282	$756,898	($707,672)	19%	$73,282	($915,412)
27	91	$756,898	27%	$75,481	$885,780	($915,412)	5%	$75,481	($1,036,663)
28	92	$885,780	-12%	$77,745	$701,741	($1,036,663)	11%	$77,745	($1,228,442)
29	93	$701,741	-16%	$80,077	$509,385	($1,228,442)	6%	$80,077	($1,382,225)
30	94	$509,385	8%	$82,480	$467,656	($1,382,225)	18%	$82,480	($1,713,506)

For instance, will you have enough money in that LIRP to withdraw if the market corrects next year? Or in five years or 10 years?

Another option is to transfer the stock market risk to an insurance company and purchase an annuity. We'll be using an index annuity in this example. Let's review the same graph as we previously used. Let's say you put in $100,000 at the beginning of that chart.

$$\begin{array}{r} \$156{,}857 \\ \times \quad 5\% \\ \hline \$7{,}842.85 \end{array}$$

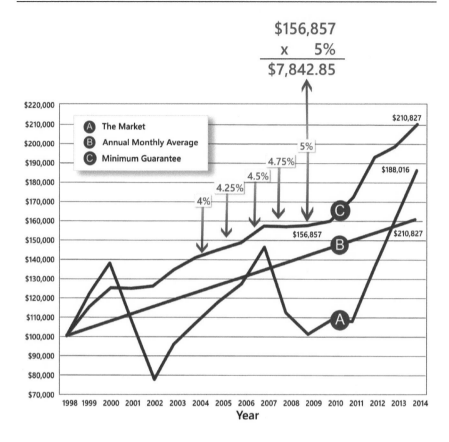

In five years, let's say the insurance company has an option that states that you'll be able to take out 4% from your portfolio. If you wait six years, it jumps up to 4.25%. In seven years, 4.5%, eight years, 4.75%. If you wait the full 10 years, you can get 5% of your money paid to you, guaranteed, for the rest of your life.

If you waited 10 years, and you got to the 5% mark, the balance now of that 100,000, is $156,857. The insurance company will multiply that balance by 5% which totals $7,842.85. So, the insurance company will pay you $7,842.85 a year guaranteed for the rest of your life, and if you have a spouse, guaranteed for the spouse's life as well. If you want those guarantees, an annuity could be the answer. You know the balance is going to be higher when you need the income because of how the indexed annuity works (gains are locked in and the principal is protected). You don't always know what it's going to be, but it will be higher. If it's in the stock market it could potentially be a lot less.

Investing in annuities: But what if you need income right away AND you can't wait to get that 5% income rate. If this is the case, then I just need to calculate how much money is needed so I can take the 10% penalty free withdrawal right away AND have enough left in 10 years, so you can have the right amount of income guaranteed for the rest of your life.

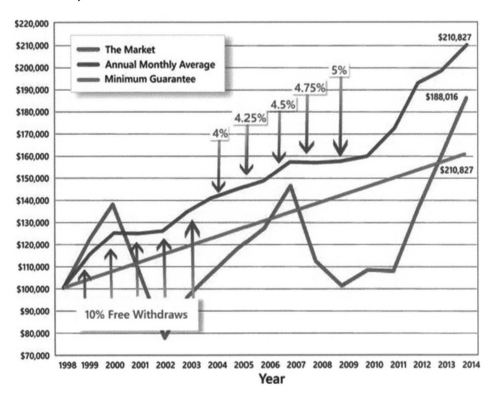

Let's assume the calculations show me that you must put in $200,000 into this annuity; then after the first year, you can start taking out 10% without any penalties or $20,000 a year to fill your gap. This would continue every year until the 5% increase feature begins. Then you can begin your guaranteed payments.

It doesn't have to be one or the other. That is why a trusted advisor can be so valuable in customizing your retirement income and financial protection. They can help create several options that will help you obtain your financial goals. Or, maybe, you use an annuity to only pay the necessities in your gap. Meaning, maybe your gap is $25,000 but that includes $10,000 of fun trips per year. The difference of $15,000 are the necessities. And anything above and beyond, or that $10,000, can be taken from the stock market if it's up for the year. If you add up your mortgage payment, your property taxes, whatever is needed to keep the lights on, whatever your core expenses are, that can be put into annuity. That's guaranteed—it's going to be paid out regardless of how long you live. And then anything above and beyond can come from your stock market portfolio. How you decide to split up your portfolio depends on your risk tolerance and how guaranteed you want income to be paid out and how much you want all this linked to the stock market.

Investing in dividend stocks: This is a stock portfolio focused on companies that pay dividends and the dividends paid are enough for your gap. First, calculate if you have enough money for this plan to work. Let's say your annual gap is $25,000. The average dividends, as I write this in April of 2018, are about 6%. If your gap is $25,000, divide 6% into that, and that's how much you need in your portfolio to build dividends to fill that gap and not touch your principal. If you see in the example below, we have social security at $36,000, a pension at $12,000, and say you want $25,000 above and beyond that for your annual income of $73,000; that can be filled by a portfolio of $416,666. Let's talk about how that works and how we got to that number.

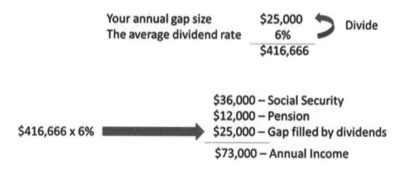

Say you take your portfolio, and just for simplicity sake, you divide it equally between these types of investments on the chart. Just to keep it general, ETFs are exchange-traded funds; they're like a mutual fund but without a money manager buying and selling securities, so the fees can be much less. Mutual funds tend to be very expensive. So, I prefer ETFs. That's what I'm going to use in this example.

Portfolio

You can use individual stocks as well; I just think that's more risk than it's worth. ETFs are baskets of stocks, so your risk is diversified. Let's say the cost of these individual ETFs allow us to buy 200 shares of the US dividend ETF, 300 shares of the European ETF, 150 shares of the increasing dividend ETF, 400 shares of preferred share ETF and 500 of a REIT ETF. We now have a portfolio of various number of shares. Each one of these shares pays a certain dividend.

Based on what each share pays and how many shares you own is how much you'll receive in dividends. For example, the top ETF could be paying us $283 a month. The second could pay $600 a month, and so on for a total of $2,083 per month. You multiply that by 12 months and there's your $25,000 gap. Again, to recap, we bought shares of ETFs that pay dividends, and now those are paying every month (some pay quarterly). We aren't touching our original $416,666 - only the dividends.

Your Portfolio		Dividend		Monthly Payout
200 shares	→	$1.415 per share	→	$283
300 shares	→	$2 per share	→	$600
150 shares	→	$2 per share	→	$300
400 shares	→	$1 per share	→	$400
500 shares	→	$1 per share	→	$500
				$2,083 per month

$2,083 x 12 months = $25,000 for your gap

Here's the important aspect that most people miss. The portfolio of $416,666 will fluctuate. If the market goes down, that portfolio's value will go down. But here's the great part: You already bought your shares. Those shares are not changing. They can't take away shares that you already own. Those shares will still pay dividends that are declared just like a paycheck.

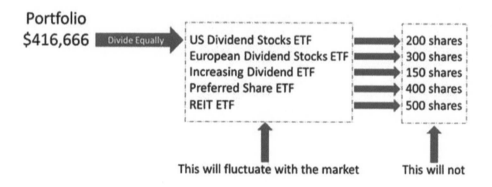

Portfolio $416,666 — Divide Equally →

US Dividend Stocks ETF → 200 shares
European Dividend Stocks ETF → 300 shares
Increasing Dividend ETF → 150 shares
Preferred Share ETF → 400 shares
REIT ETF → 500 shares

This will fluctuate with the market   This will not

Yes, companies you own through these ETFs may decrease dividends, but I can tell you from doing this for almost 20 years, it's not going to happen very often. When they do go down, it's not very much. In each of these ETFs, you may own 200-300 companies each, so the risk of that is diversified. Again, your portfolio could fluctuate, but your income will not. It will be like a paycheck just like when you worked. But if it causes stress, that your portfolio's going down, then maybe a dividend portfolio is not right for you.

Here's a recap: Let's say our social security is $36,000 and our pension is $12,000. So your gap is $25,000. Consider the stock market to fill that gap if your gap is 3% or less of your portfolio balance, and you're comfortable with stock market volatility. This strategy is best if you have backup money to use when the market is down—like a LIRP. So that percentage may be much higher.

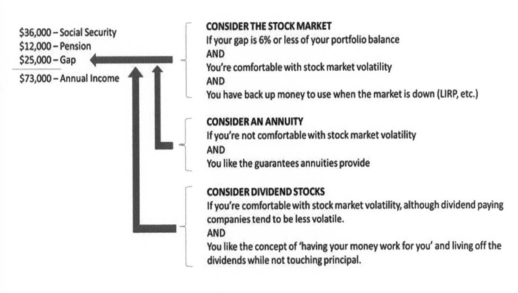

$36,000 – Social Security
$12,000 – Pension
$25,000 – Gap
$73,000 – Annual Income

CONSIDER THE STOCK MARKET
If your gap is 6% or less of your portfolio balance
AND
You're comfortable with stock market volatility
AND
You have back up money to use when the market is down (LIRP, etc.)

CONSIDER AN ANNUITY
If you're not comfortable with stock market volatility
AND
You like the guarantees annuities provide

CONSIDER DIVIDEND STOCKS
If you're comfortable with stock market volatility, although dividend paying companies tend to be less volatile.
AND
You like the concept of 'having your money work for you' and living off the dividends while not touching principal.

Consider an annuity if you're not comfortable with stock market volatility and you like the guarantees that annuities provide and you don't mind that access to your money is limited for the tradeoff of those guarantees. Consider dividend stocks if you're comfortable with stock market volatility and you like the concept of having your money work for you and living off the dividends while not touching your principal. Your money is 100% liquid, unlike an annuity, but if you sell any stocks then your income will go down because you sold shares that were generating your income. That's why sometimes it's alright that the portfolio goes down if you can wait it out; if you don't need access to that money, just let it keep paying you dividends. Let it come back up in value. But again, that's not for everybody. There are pros and cons of each one of these strategies. Which is why I highly recommend contacting me or having a trusted advisor to help you create a retirement package that fits your financial goals.

ESTATE PLANNING

W e've discussed building an income plan and protecting it from an unplanned long-term care event. Now, let's discuss setting up a plan to pass it on to heirs properly. A will is a document that states your final wishes but does not avoid probate court. An attorney must still take your will down to probate court and convince the judge that it is indeed your last will and testament. The main reason for a will are as follows:

1. Leave instructions about what should happen to your belongings if you die.
2. You want to name an executor.
3. You want to name guardians for your children and their belongings.
4. You want to decide how debts and taxes are going to be paid.
5. You want to provide for pets

You shouldn't try to use a will to put conditions on your gifts—like I give my house to Susan if she finishes college. A will is basic, but it can be useful.

I usually recommend everyone has a will *and* a trust. A living revocable trust is like setting up a company where you and your spouse are the executors of this company. Living, means you create it while you're alive. Revocable means you can change it at any time while you're alive and trust is just the type of document that it is. A living revocable trust is what most people ought to have. It avoids probate unlike a will. It plans for the possibility of your own incapacity. Most remember the Terri Schiavo case. From 1990 to 2015—she was in various stages of consciousness and could not make any decisions nor sign any documents. A trust with certain provisions could avoid this from happening by clearly documenting who is in charge and by what parameters.

Really, the worst-case scenario is not that you die. When you die, with proper planning, things are clear what's going to happen. But when you don't die, and you're incapacitated and unable to talk, that's when key financial aspects need to be spelled out and a trust is the way to do that.

A living revocable trust can:

1. Control what happens to your real estate after you're gone; wills are not appropriate for controlling your real estate.
2. Prevent your financial affairs from becoming public. Part of probate opens your financial affairs to the public.
3. Avoid recovery by your state. Many people aren't aware that if Medicaid is used to pay for your spouse to be in a nursing home, after you and your spouse dies, the state could come after your estate for recovery of whatever money they spent for care. They can only do this if your estate is transferred outside of a trust. If it goes through probate, the state has the rights to recover money spent via your assets. But this can't occur if it is transferred using a trust.
4. Avoid creditor issues when your child inherits your IRAs. If your child inherits your IRA, it's no longer protected from creditors. That occurred with a recent IRS ruling. The IRS decided that once it's inherited it is no longer a 'retirement account' and is exposed to creditors. Consult your lawyer or attorney if you have that issue.

Your will and trust should work together. For instance, you want to make sure your will has a 'pour-over' clause. That means if you forgot to put something into the trust or name something in your trust, and you die, the 'pour-over' clause states that the item belongs in your trust.

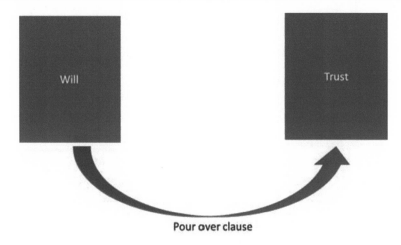

Pour over clause

After you set up a trust, you need to name the trust as either your main or contingent beneficiaries on your beneficiary forms. Each case is different, and a qualified estate planning attorney can advise you on the proper set up. For non-IRA accounts, and other assets without beneficiaries, you'll usually want to change the ownership from individual people to the name of the trust. For qualified accounts, like IRAs and 401Ks, you can usually name the spouse as the main beneficiary, and then if something happens to both of you, the contingent beneficiary is the trust. You usually don't want to name the trust as the main beneficiary unless you're single. You want the spouse to have the most control when you die. But if something happens to both of you, you want the trust to take over. You should consult an attorney to verify if that is the best decision for you.

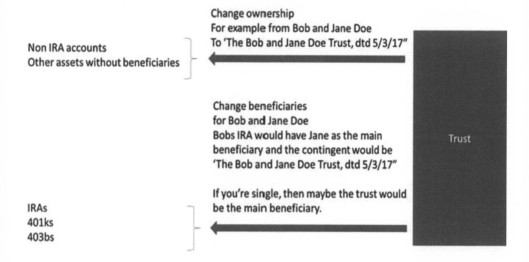

What's the best way to get a will? I don't mind sites like www.legalzoom.com. They can get it done and it's inexpensive. But for a trust, you really need to consult an attorney. They're just too complex to be handled by a general website.

MEDICAID PLANNING

M edicaid planning is complex. I want to convey the main concepts, so you can go to an elder law attorney if any of it applies to you. Let's go over some of these strategies. What's Medicaid planning in the first place? A general definition is: any assistance provided to a potential Medicaid applicant in advance of and preparation for their Medicaid application. In layman's terms, you try to hide assets legally, so the government will pay for your nursing home care or in-home care. Medicaid planning can be as simple as assistance with the collection and preparation of documents or as complicated as a complete restructuring of one's financial assets.

Let's look at an example for a married couple. Regarding the picture below, let's say you have $100,000 in assets. Then the spouse enters a nursing home. Currently, 32 states calculate whether you qualify for Medicaid in this manner. Michigan happens to be one of them.

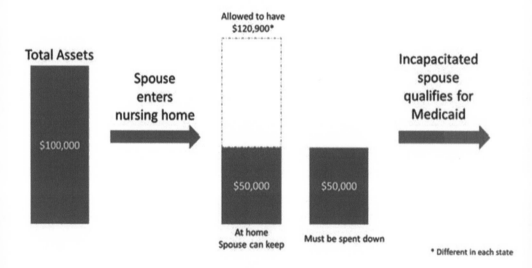

The calculation is as follows: They divide your total assets in half, on the day you entered the nursing home. Whatever amount is above the current figure of $120,900 (this figure can change annually) must be spent down before Medicaid will begin paying for long-term care. Your home, one car and a burial plot is not counted. The spend down amount can be spent down many ways. It can be put into a home for repairs or upgrades because a home is a non-counted asset. But beyond that, many times the spend down is more money than people can or want to invest into their home. So, let's follow this example to avoid that. Assume you have $100,000 in countable assets and your spouse enters a nursing home. The state splits the amount in half so $50,000 can be kept by the spouse that's still at home and $50,000 must be spent down. It must be depleted somehow. Put it into the home or have it spent down some other way but it cannot be gifted to anyone or that will extend the period to which you will not qualify for Medicaid.

Once the proper amount is spent down or spent on care, the incapacitated spouse now qualifies for Medicaid. The spouse at home has $50,000 left. But they're allowed to have $120,900, so this is where this next strategy comes in. Let's start by looking at the tall column titled, "Total Assets" that is $100,000. Because the home is not a countable asset, and you're allowed to transfer as much money from spouse to spouse, we're going to temporarily take a home equity loan and take $141,800 out of the home and put it into the client's assets.

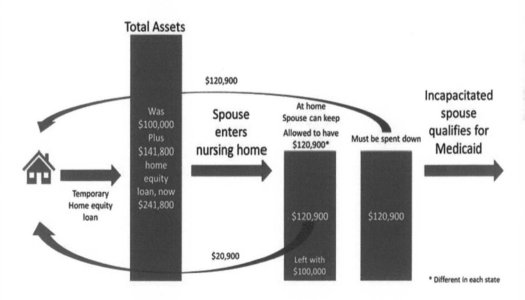

They had $100,000 but we're going to now add in a home equity loan of $141,800. They now have $241,800 in assets.

Now follow the arrow to the right. The spouse enters the nursing home, so the state performs the calculation by splitting your assets in half. Now, half of $241,800 is $120,900. The maximum that the 'at home' spouse can keep. So, half of that is $120,900 (can be kept by the spouse) and $120,900 (needs to be spent down). We're just going to use the proceeds from the home equity loan to pay off the home equity loan. That leaves us with $100,000, our original assets we are trying to protect. We basically just took a home equity loan out and added that to our assets temporarily. Medicaid told us we had to spend down half of the money, so we reversed the home equity loan so it's 'spent down'.

Using this strategy, we are now able to keep double what we had before we did the strategy. The 'at-home' spouse was only allowed to keep $50,000 before but because we temporarily added money to our asset bucket, we can keep $100,000, not just $50,000. Now that the money is 'spent down' and we're left with $100,000, the incapacitated spouse qualifies for Medicaid. Consult an elder law attorney and talk to them about this strategy.

The other technique is called 'half-a-loaf' technique. This is a complicated strategy and an experienced elder law attorney must be used. This works well for a single person. Let's say you have $200,000 in assets. You divide your assets roughly in half and gift it away to whomever (children, grandchildren, etc.).

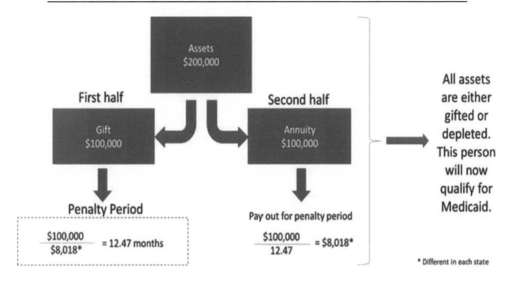

Here's what a lot of people don't understand: the penalty look-back period is five years, but if you did gift money in that five years, then you must go to the next step to calculate the penalty period. If you gift a small amount one year before you enter a nursing home, the penalty period may only be one month. Meaning, you'll have to pay out-of-pocket for one month before Medicaid begins paying.

The penalty period is calculated by dividing how much you gifted into the average monthly nursing home stay in your state. In the state of Michigan, it happens to currently be $8,018 a month (this can change annually). You can search the internet or contact an elder law attorney to find out what it is for your state. So, in our example, $100,000 (our gift) divided by the $8,018 gives you a penalty period of 12.47 months. That's how long you must pay for care yourself as a penalty for gifting half your portfolio.

So, the first half of $100,000 was gifted and you have a penalty period of 12.47 months. Now let's deal with the second half. You place that into a special annuity to pay for the 12.47 penalty period. So, to continue this example, let's say you go into a nursing home, and your payout from of this annuity is $8,018 a month. After 12.47 months, that money is gone and now Medicaid considers the gifting period is over simultaneously as planned. And now you have 'spent down' the assets and you can qualify for Medicaid. Yet you were able to gift $100,000 to your children or grandchildren just over one year prior. That's a great strategy that many don't know. A good elder law care attorney will know this and be able to work out all these numbers for you.

I hope you enjoyed this high-level recap of how I take prospects through each aspect of income planning from social security to protecting it at the end of life. I enjoy educating so keep an eye on my website for where I'll be speaking next. You can also visit www.baby-boomerclass.com to take my free video online class to build your own retirement income plan. My youtube channel has many videos located at www.youtube.com/bridgeriveradvisors.